About This Book

Title: *Plants*

Step: 2

Word Count: 107

Skills in Focus: L-blends

Tricky Words: grow, flower, make, bloom, water, fall, some

Ideas For Using This Book

Before Reading:
- **Comprehension:** Look at the title and cover image together. Walk through the pictures in the book with readers and have them make predictions about what they might learn in the book. Help them make connections by asking what they already know about plants.
- **Accuracy:** Practice saying the tricky words listed on page 1.
- **Phonemic Awareness:** Explain to readers that a blend is two consonants together that each make a sound. Discuss that some blends include the letter *L*. Read aloud story words containing L-blends, beginning with *plant*. Segment the sounds slowly and have the students call out the word. Call attention to each blend and where it is found within the word. Other words to practice: *plum, black, plot*.

During Reading:
- Have readers point under each word as they read it.
- **Decoding:** If readers are stuck on a word, help them say each sound and blend the sounds together smoothly. Be sure to point out L-blends as they appear.
- **Comprehension:** Invite students to talk about what new things they are learning about plants while reading. What are they learning that they didn't know before?

After Reading:
Discuss the book. Some ideas for questions:
- Where do plants grow? What plants have you seen?
- How can you take care of plants?
- What do you still wonder about plants?

Plants

Text by Laura Stickney

Reading Consultant
Deborah MacPhee, PhD
Professor, School of Teaching and Learning
Illinois State University

PICTURE WINDOW BOOKS
a capstone imprint

Plants grow in lots of spots. You can put plants in flat plots.

Flowers are plants.

Plums bud on plants.

Plants must get sun.

Plants get big in the sun.

Plants must get wet.
Put water in a can.

Let it fall on plants. Plip plop!

Red buds will bloom on plants.

Bugs flock to plants. Slugs slip on flat plants.

Some bugs can help plants. Bugs flit and flap.

One bud is black.
It has a slim stem.

It will not get big.

Let's clip it off. Snip snip!

Black buds drop.

Pluck a red flower.

Pluck a big red plum.

21

Plants can make us glad.

More Ideas:

Phonemic Awareness Activity

Practicing L-Blends:
Tell readers they will segment the sounds of story words containing L-blends. Say an L-blend word for the readers to segment the sounds. They will slowly stretch out the sounds of each word, tapping the table as they produce each sound.

Suggested words:
- plant
- slip
- plum
- black

Extended Learning Activity

Plant Scavenger Hunt:
Have readers go outside and help them look for different types of plants. Ask them to make drawings of the plants they see. Or, ask readers to write a list of the plants they see. Ask readers about how the plants are similar and different.

Published by Picture Window Books, an imprint of Capstone
1710 Roe Crest Drive, North Mankato, Minnesota 56003
capstonepub.com

Copyright © 2026 by Capstone.
All rights reserved. No part of this publication may be reproduced
in whole or in part, or stored in a retrieval system, or transmitted in
any form or by any means, electronic, mechanical, photocopying,
recording, or otherwise, without written permission of the publisher.

Library of Congress Cataloging-in-Publication Data is available
on the Library of Congress website.

ISBN: 9798875226984 (hardback)
ISBN: 9798875229664 (paperback)
ISBN: 9798875229640 (eBook PDF)

Image Credits: iStock: Akarawut Lohacharoenvanich, 22-23, amenic181, 2-3, brytta, cover, cjp, 4-5, keepphotos, 18-19, Pradip Singh, 16-17, Six_Characters, 10; Shutterstock: anmbph, 12-13, Fotohunter, 8-9, Jesse Franks, 14-15, 24, LutsenkoLarissa, 1, 6, pavla, 20, Tatevosian Yana, 21, Tetiana Matsko, 7, wavebreakmedia, 11

Printed and bound in China. PO 6274